Getting Around

By Boat

Cassie Mayer

Heinemann Library
Chicago, Illinois

© 2006 Heinemann Library
a division of Reed Elsevier Inc.
Chicago, Illinois

Customer Service 888–454–2279

Visit our website at www.heinemannlibrary.com

Photo research by Tracy Cummins
Designed by Jo Hinton-Malivoire
Printed and bound in China by South China Printing Company
10 09 08 07 06
10 9 8 7 6 5 4 3 2

Library of Congress Cataloging-in-Publication Data
Mayer, Cassie.
  By boat / Cassie Mayer.— 1st ed.
      p. cm. — (Getting around)
  Includes bibliographical references and index.
  ISBN 1-4034-8389-2 (hc) — ISBN 1-4034-8396-5 (pb)
  1. Ships—Juvenile literature. 2. Boats and boating—Juvenile literature.
I. Title. II. Series.
  VM150.M39 2006-
  623.82—dc22
    2785   2005036558

Acknowledgments
The author and publisher are grateful to the following for permission to reproduce copyright material:
Alamy p. **22** (Image DJ); Corbis pp. **4** (Lester Lefkowitz), **5** (Frans Lemmens/zefa), **6** (Charles & Josette Lenars), **7** (Chris Lisle), **8** (Onne van der Wal), **9** (Setboun), **10** (Tom Stewart), **11** (Xiaoyang Liu), **12** (Owen Franken), **14** (ML Sinibaldi), **16** (Royalty Free), **17** (Onne van der Wal), **18** (Tom Stewart), **19** (William Manning), **21** (Rob Howard), **23** (fisherman, Tom Stewart), **23** (barge, Charles & Josette Lenars), **23** (motor boat, Onne van der Wal), **23** (ferry boat, Xiaoyang Liu); Getty Images pp. **13** (Streano), **15** (Frerck), **20** (Puddy).

Cover image of a river boat reproduced with permission of Hubert Stadler/Corbis. Backcover image of a barge reproduced with permission of Charles & Josette Lenars.

Special thanks to Margo Browne for her help with this project.

Contents

Getting Around by Boat

Every day people move from place to place.

Some people move by boat.

What Boats Carry

cargo

Boats carry cargo.

Boats carry people.

How Boats Move

Some boats use motors to move.

Other boats use wind to move.

Riding on Boats

captain

A captain drives the boat.

People ride on boats.

Types of Boats

wood

Some boats are made of wood.

steel

Other boats are made of steel.

How People Use Boats

People sell food from boats.

People catch fish from boats.

People ride in boats for fun.

Some people race boats.

Boats can take you to far away places.

Boats can take you to places close by.

Some people ride in boats
all alone.

But it is fun to invite friends along!

Boat Vocabulary

motor

windshield

stern (back)

bow (front)

Picture Glossary

 **captain** a person who drives a boat

 **cargo** a large group of items

 **motor** a machine that makes a boat move

Index

Notes to Parents and Teachers

Boats are a form of transportation familiar to children, but how are boats used throughout the world? The photographs in this book expand children's horizons by showing how people move from place to place by boat. Some of the locations featured are Washington (page 4), Florida (page 17), Peru (page 5, cover), India (page 6), Thailand (pages 7, 14), China (pages 9, 11), France (page 12), Mexico (page 15), Greenland (page 18), Italy (page 19), Vietnam (page 20), and New Guinea (page 21).

The text has been chosen with the advice of a literacy expert to enable beginning readers success reading independently or with moderate support. An expert in the field of early childhood social studies education was consulted to ensure developmentally appropriate content.

You can support children's nonfiction literacy skills by helping them use the table of contents, headings, picture glossary, and index.